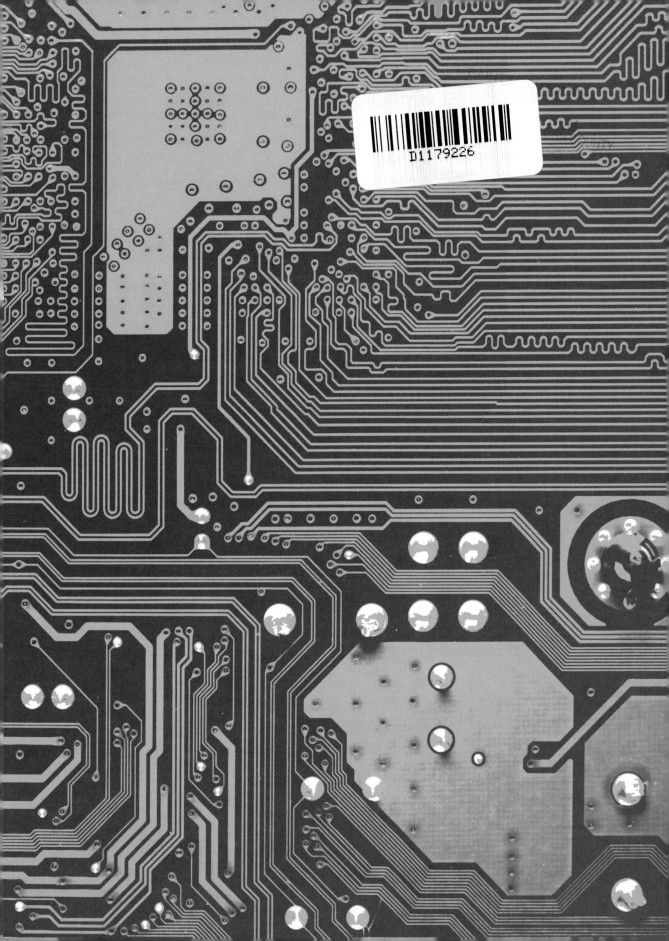

D1179226

BAINTE DEN STOC

WITHDRAWN FROM
DÚN LAOGHAIRE-RATHDOWN COUNTY
LIBRARY STOCK

# TRIUMPHS OF TECHNOLOGY

WAYLAND
www.waylandbooks.co.uk

DÚN LAOGHAIRE-
RATHDOWN LIBRARIES

| DLR27000029766 | |
| --- | --- |
| BERTRAMS | 14/11/2018 |
| | |
| GR | 02366436 |

First published in Great Britain
in 2018 by Wayland
Copyright © Hodder & Stoughton, 2018

Wayland
An imprint of Hachette
Children's Group
Part of Hodder & Stoughton
Carmelite House
50 Victoria Embankment
London EC4Y 0DZ

All rights reserved

Series editor: Elise Short
Produced by Tall Tree Ltd
Written by: Rob Colson
Designer: Ben Ruocco

ISBN: 978 1 5263 08375

10 9 8 7 6 5 4 3 2 1

An Hachette UK Company
www.hachette.co.uk
www.hachettechildrens.co.uk

Printed and bound in China

The website addresses (URLs) included in this
book were valid at the time of going to press.
However, it is possible that contents or addresses
may have changed since the publication of this
book. No responsibility for any such changes can
be accepted by either the author or the Publisher.

MIX
Paper from
responsible sources
FSC
www.fsc.org    FSC® C104740

**Picture credits**
t–top, b–bottom, l–left, r–right, c–centre,
front cover–fc, back cover–bc
All images courtesy of Dreamstime.com and all
icons made by Freepik from www.flaticon.com,
unless indicated:

Inside front Elena11/Shutterstock;; fc, bc Deviney;
fcr, 12-13 Ezumeimages; fcbl Scanrail;
fcbl Aprescindere; fcbl, 26br Leonardo255; bcl,
12bl Library of Congress; bcl, 22cl MGM/Clarence
Bull; bcl, 14cr Library and Archives Canada;
4-5 Johns Hopkins University Applied Physics
Laboratory; 5br Grendelkhan/Attribution-
ShareAlike 4.0 International (CC BY-SA 4.0);
6-7 Olegdudko; 7tr 22tomtom; 8c Vvostal; 9br
Ivansmuk; 9br Valery Lisin; 10br Aprescindere;
11tr Everett Collection Inc.; 14bl National Archives
and Records Administration; 14-15 Cowardlion;
15br Jiripravda; 17b Smashicons; 19t Pattarapong
Kumlert; 20l Library of Congress; 20br Hzeller/
Attribution-ShareAlike 3.0 Unported (CC BY-SA
3.0); 21t Mikhail Basov; 21t Sswartz; 22–23
Dvmsimages; 24bl Enrique Dans/ Attribution 2.0
Generic (CC BY 2.0); 24–25 Pressureua;
26bl Redrum0486/Attribution-ShareAlike 3.0
Unported (CC BY-SA 3.0); 26bc Dmitry Kazantsev;
26cr Joseph Brophy; 27bl Krystyna Wojciechowska
– Czarnik; 28bl US Naval Research Laboratory;
28–29 NOAA; 29t Andrey Yaroslavtsev/
Shutterstock; 29br marrishuanna/Shutterstock;
31br Reservoir Dots/Shutterstock.

Every effort has been made to acknowledge every
image source but the publisher apologises for any
unintentional errors or omissions that will be
corrected in future editions of this book.

# CONTENTS

# TECHNOLOGY RULES THE WORLD

We have created all kinds of technology to help us to do our work. The first technology took the form of simple tools that were made by hand by one or two people. The latest technology requires thousands of people to make it. It is designed and run using computers, performing tasks that would have been unimaginable just a few decades ago.

## Simple machines

The earliest technology made use of six simple machines. These machines make work easier by changing the size or direction of a force. They enable someone to do the same work with less effort.

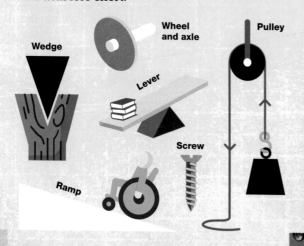

Wedge

Wheel and axle

Pulley

Lever

Screw

Ramp

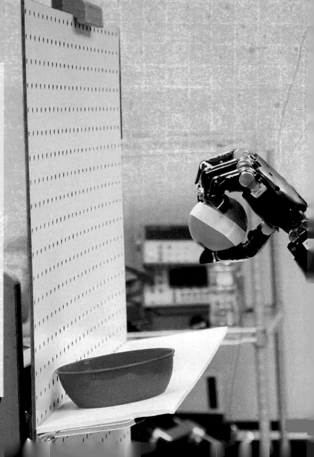

## Ancient technology

Much of the earliest technology was developed to help farmers. The Archimedes screw was invented 3,000 years ago. It raises water from streams into fields to grow crops. As the screw is turned, water is scooped up at the bottom and pushed up through a tube to the top. Farmers still use Archimedes screws today.

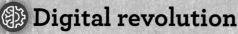

## Digital revolution

**Modern technology is driven by ever-improving computers, which not only control machines, but can also design them.**

## Man and machine

Robotic arms and legs have been developed for people who lost limbs to illness or accidents. The artificial limbs, known as prostheses, can be linked to nerves that lead to the brain. This allows the wearer to control the limbs using their thoughts.

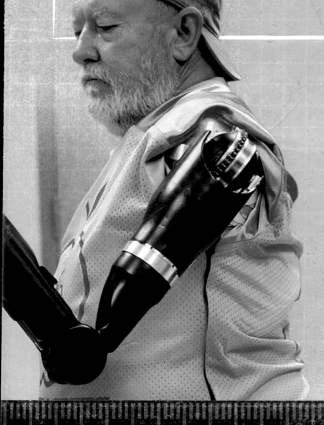

## The present and the future

Computer technology has created a new generation of machines that can learn from experience. Self-driving cars are currently being tested on private roads to ready them for use on public roads. As they drive, the cars learn from each new experience, updating their systems to show the best course of action. In the future, our roads may be filled with driverless cars, which could save many lives by reducing accidents.

Google's Waymo driverless car finds its way using a system called Lidar, which bounces laser beams off its surroundings.

**Read on to discover the technological challenges inventors have overcome. The answers to questions in the projects are found on page 31.**

# CREATING A CURRENT

A battery is a store of chemical energy that produces an electric current when it is linked up to a circuit. The first battery was made in 1799 by Italian inventor Alessandro Volta.

### Alessandro Volta (1745–1827)

Volta made his battery by building up layers of zinc and copper, separated by cloth soaked in salt water. When he connected the top and bottom of his battery with a wire, an electric current flowed through it. Named after its inventor, the first battery was known as a voltaic pile.

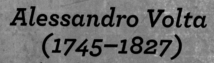

Volta's battery created an electric charge using cells of zinc, copper and salt water.

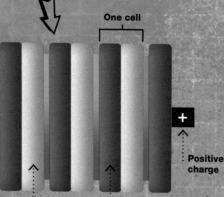

Negative charge

One cell

−

+

Positive charge

Salt water    Zinc    Copper

## How did it work?

Volta did not fully understand how his battery worked. Today we know that electricity is created by the flow of tiny particles called electrons. Electrons have a negative charge and flow towards a place with a positive charge. A battery has a positive terminal and a negative terminal, separated by a chemical called an electrolyte. In Volta's battery, a chemical reaction between the zinc and the salt water produced a negative charge in the zinc plate. Electrons entered the salt water at the copper plate. This set up a flow of electrons around the wire from the zinc plate to the copper plate.

Modern batteries all work according to the same basic principle as the voltaic pile.

## Recharging

A battery can be recharged by reversing the chemical reaction in the electrolyte. Electrons flow towards the negative terminal to restore the battery's power. The batteries of electric cars can be recharged by plugging them in to on-street charging points. They can drive up to 200 kilometres on one charge.

## PROJECT: ICE CUBE TRAY BATTERY

**Power an LED with this homemade battery.**

**You will need:** an ice cube tray, five galvanised nails, five pieces of copper wire, distilled vinegar, an LED

1. Wrap a length of wire around the top of each nail so that some wire hangs down the side.
2. Fill the first six cells of the tray with vinegar. Straddle the LED across the first two cells.
3. Place a nail in one of the first two cells so that the copper wire dips into the next cell. Place the next nail in that cell and drape the wire into the next one, and repeat until the last piece of copper dips into the cell with the LED.

The LED should light up. If you have more nails and wire, try making a battery using more of the cells. Does the LED shine more brightly?

# CAPTURING AN IMAGE

Photographs fix images of the world for us to look at forever. Photography technology has evolved from the grainy black-and-white photographs of the 19th century to the high-definition colour images of today.

## ⚙ Camera obscura

Photography was invented in the early 19th century using a device called a camera obscura (Latin for 'dark room'). The camera obscura projected an image on to a screen by letting light into a dark box through a small hole. Photographs were created by coating the screen with light-sensitive chemicals to fix the image.

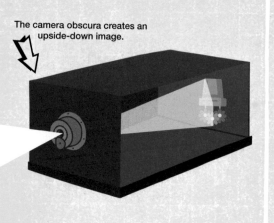

The camera obscura creates an upside-down image.

## *Nicéphore Niépce (1795–1833)*

The oldest surviving photograph was taken by French inventor Niépce in 1826. He captured an image of the view from his window (see right). Niépce had to expose the screen to the light for several hours to create the image, so it was only possible to capture a still-life.

## Portrait photography

By the mid-19th century, photography technology had improved, and new chemicals made it possible to fix an image with much shorter exposure times. This allowed photographers to take photos of people. British photographer Julia Margaret Cameron (1815–1879) was a pioneer in portrait photography, producing images with a high level of detail.

Cameron took this photo of a young girl called Annie in 1864.

## Thermal imaging

Light is a kind of radiation called electromagnetic radiation. Our eyes see only visible light, but some cameras can detect other forms of radiation. Warm objects such as bodies give off infrared radiation, which is invisible to our eyes. Night vision cameras sense infrared and turn it into images that we can see. This is called thermal imaging.

Engineers use thermal imaging to check that machines are working correctly. The different colours represent different temperatures.

## *Going digital*

Modern digital cameras project an image on to light detectors that turn the image into electrical signals. The image can then be stored on the camera's memory.

### PROJECT:
# INVISIBLE BEAMS

Remote controls for televisions or other equipment work by sending beams of radiation. We cannot see these beams, but the digital cameras on mobile phones can pick them up.

**You will need:** TV remote control, mobile phone

Place a remote control in front of a phone's camera and press some buttons on the remote control.

Do you see light flashing on the image on the phone's screen? The flashes you are seeing are infrared beams.

# SENDING A MESSAGE

Before the discovery of electricity at the end of the 18th century, it took days to send a message from one part of a country to another, and weeks to send one to a different part of the world. The electronic telegraph allowed messages called telegrams to be sent almost instantly.

## Samuel Morse (1791–1872)

By the 1830s, many inventors around the world were experimenting with ways to send electrical signals along a wire. American inventor Samuel Morse created one of the first commercially useful telegraph systems. His system sent pulses of electricity along a single wire. Morse sent his first message over five kilometres of wire in 1838.

## Morse code

Telegraph systems transmit messages as a series of pulses. Samuel Morse created a code for his telegraph system that is still in use today. Morse code translates letters and numbers using a combination of short pulses (dots) and long pulses (dashes).

# Worldwide network

From the 1850s onwards, telegraph wires were laid across oceans. In 1902, a line across the Pacific finally encircled the world. Almost instant worldwide communications were now possible.

Telegraph operators were highly skilled in sending and receiving coded messages.

## International distress signal

Since 1908, 'SOS' has been the standard international distress signal in Morse code. The message is a continuous sequence of three dots followed by three dashes, and was chosen as it is easily recognisable even to people who are not trained in Morse code.

## PROJECT:
## TELEGRAPH SET

With the help of an adult, you can make your own telegraph set.

**You will need:** a 9V battery, three wooden boards, copper wire, insulated electric wire, a thin copper plate, a thin steel plate, a galvanised nail, screws, screwdriver

1. To make the transmitter, first secure with a screw the strip of copper bent upwards over a screw on a wooden board.
2. To make the receiver, you first need to create an electromagnet. You do this by wrapping copper wire around a nail. Secure the nail on a board, and fix another board at right angles to it. Secure the steel strip hanging over the nail, as shown.
3. Connect the transmitter and receiver to the battery using the electric wires, as shown.

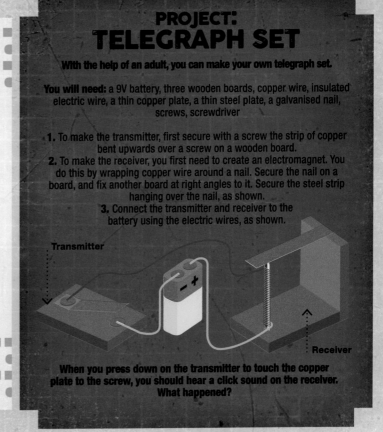

Transmitter

Receiver

When you press down on the transmitter to touch the copper plate to the screw, you should hear a click sound on the receiver. What happened?

# LIGHTING OUR HOMES

The first electric light bulb was made by British inventor Humphrey Davy in 1802. He passed a current through a piece of carbon, which glowed brightly. However, Davy's bulb broke quickly and was far too bright to light a home. The first practical light bulb was made more than 70 years later by American Thomas Edison.

## Thomas Edison (1847–1931)

Edison's light bulb worked in a similar way to Davy's: making a thin thread-like filament glow by passing electricity through it. This is called an incandescent light bulb. After experimenting with many different materials, Edison discovered that a filament made from carbonised bamboo would last for hundreds of hours before breaking. He set to work mass-producing his bulb.

Incandescent light bulb ⇨

# How does it work?

In an incandescent light bulb, as electricity passes through the filament, it resists the current in a way that causes it to heat up and glow brightly.

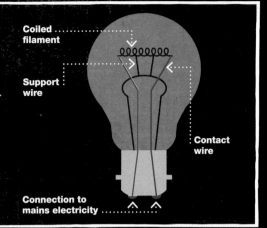

Coiled filament

Support wire

Contact wire

Connection to mains electricity

## Saving energy

More than 90 per cent of the energy needed to power an incandescent light bulb produces heat rather than light. In recent years, they have been replaced by more efficient bulbs.

Fluorescent light bulbs produce light by passing an electric current through a gas. LED bulbs produce light by passing a current through a material called a semiconductor.

Fluorescent light bulbs are many times more efficient than incandescent bulbs.

LED light bulbs are even more efficient than fluorescent light bulbs.

## PROJECT:
# MAKE A LIGHT BULB

**You will need:** A large canning jar with a lid, 9-volt battery, 1 metre of insulated copper wire, thin iron wire (such as unravelled picture-hanging wire)

Battery

Copper wire

Iron wire

**1.** Ask an adult to cut the copper wire in half and strip about 3 cm of the insulation off the ends of each piece. Ask an adult to punch two holes in the jar lid with a nail. Thread one end of each copper wire through the hole.

**2.** Make a hook on each end of the copper wire that will be inside the jar. Twist three strands of the iron wire together, then twist the ends around the hooks in the copper wire. This will be your filament.

**3.** Place the lid on the jar and carefully connect the free ends of the copper wire to each terminal on the battery. After connecting the battery, be careful not to touch the iron wire as it will get very hot.

**What colour light does your bulb give off?**

# TALKING ON THE LINE

While the telegraph could send messages a long distance, it could only transmit simple signals such as Morse code. In the 1870s, many inventors across the world were working on a way to transmit human voices across wires.

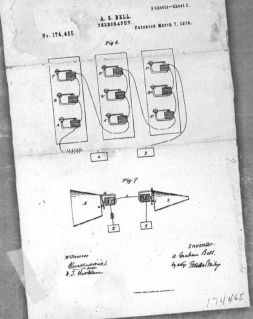

## *Alexander Graham Bell (1847–1922)*

Although many others claimed to have invented the telephone before him, Scottish-born Alexander Graham Bell was the first to make a practical version. Working in Boston, USA, Bell found a way to turn the vibrations produced by the human voice into a varying electric current, which could then be carried over a telegraph line.

Bell submitted this drawing of his telephone to the US Patent Office in 1876. The patent prevented others from using his invention without his permission. It caused a bitter disagreement with rival inventor Elisha Gray, who accused Bell of stealing his idea.

## How it works

A telephone converts sound into electricity and back into sound. A vibrating membrane called a diaphragm in the mouthpiece converts sound energy into an electrical current. The current travels along a line to the earpiece of the receiver. A diaphragm in the earpiece turns the electrical energy back into sound energy.

## Making a connection

When you make a telephone call on a landline, the number you dial tells the switchboard which line you wish to connect to and temporarily connects you up to the number you are calling. The first telephone switchboards were operated manually. A person first phoned an operator and told them the number they wished to be connected to. The operator would then manually move the lines by plugging them into different sockets on a wooden board. Today, switchboards are operated by computer.

## PROJECT:
# MAKE A STRING TELEPHONE

**See how sounds can be transmitted as vibrations across a string.**

**You will need:** Two large paper or disposable plastic cups, two paperclips, 10-metre-long cotton string or fishing line, a friend and a quiet area

**1.** Ask an adult to use a nail to punch a small hole in the centre of the bottom of both cups. Thread one end of string through the bottom of each cup.
**2.** Place a paperclip in each cup and tie the string around it. (This is just there to hold the string in place.)
**3.** Give one cup to your friend and walk slowly apart until the string is tight.
**4.** Hold the cup over your ear and ask your friend to talk into their cup, then reverse roles.

**Can you hear your friend clearly? Try again but letting the string go slack, or with a third person standing in the middle, holding the string. What happens?**

# AIRWAVE BROADCASTING

Radios work by receiving messages in the form of radio waves, which carry information that they turn into sound or pictures (see pages 20–21).

## Guglielmo Marconi
### (1874–1937)

Italian inventor Guglielmo Marconi developed a wireless telegraph that sent messages in Morse code (see page 11) by radio waves. Due to a lack of interest in Italy, Marconi took his idea to Britain, where he found eager investors. The first wireless telegraph was set up in 1898 between a lighthouse and a lightship in the English Channel. Two years later, Marconi successfully sent a radio signal across the Atlantic Ocean. Radios were soon fitted to large ships. When the ship *Titanic* hit an iceberg in 1912, a radio message alerted rescuers to come to its aid.

16

# Sound broadcasting

In 1900, Brazilian priest Roberto Landell was the first person to broadcast a human voice by radio. Twenty years later, a radio station in Buenos Aires, Argentina, broadcast a live opera performance. Only 20 homes in the city had receivers capable of picking up the broadcast, but just a few years later, radio had become a truly mass means of communication.

Radio transmitters code sound waves into a varying electrical current. The current passes through an antenna, where electrons are made to vibrate. This vibration produces radio waves.

The radio waves make electrons in the receiver's antenna vibrate. This produces an electric current with the same pattern as the transmitter's current. The receiver decodes the pattern to turn the electrical current into sound.

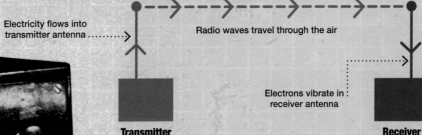

Electricity flows into transmitter antenna .........

Radio waves travel through the air

Electrons vibrate in receiver antenna

**Transmitter**

**Receiver**

By 1915, Marconi was manufacturing powerful radio receivers for wireless telegraphy stations. The Type 106 pictured here could pick up Morse code messages that had been transmitted thousands of kilometres away.

## PROJECT:
# MAKE A METAL DETECTOR

See how radio waves can be used to detect metal.

**You will need:** An old battery-powered portable radio with AM and FM bands, a small battery-powered calculator (not solar-powered), batteries for both devices, duct tape

**1.** Switch the radio to AM and turn the dial far to the right so that you only hear static. Turn the volume up high.
**2.** Turn on the calculator and hold it to the radio so that the battery compartments are touching. Holding the two together, place them close to a metal object. If they are aligned correctly, you will hear a change in the static to a beeping sound. If you don't hear the beeps, adjust the position of the calculator until you do. Tape the radio and calculator together in this position.
**3.** Test out your metal detector on other objects.

**How do you think this works?**

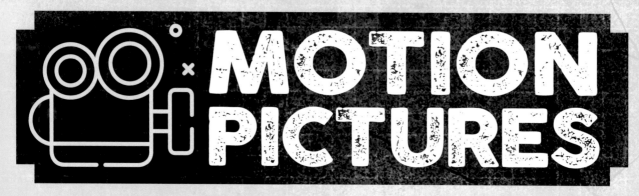

# MOTION PICTURES

Motion pictures, or movies, create the illusion of a moving image from a series of still images, or frames.

## Eadweard Muybridge (1830–1904)

In the 1870s, English photographer Eadweard Muybridge produced some of the earliest motion pictures. Muybridge set up a series of 12 cameras to photograph a horse in a sequence of shots, which he put together to create a moving image. One short movie played the first eleven frames below one after the other, revealing for the first time how a horse's legs move when it gallops.

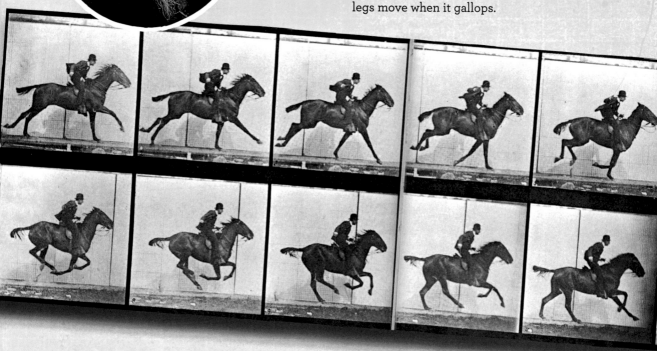

## Optical illusion

Movie projectors work by separately showing 24 different frames per second. The feeling of movement is an optical illusion, as the rapidly changing images fool our brains into thinking that we are seeing motion.

For old movies, a film reel with the sequence of frames was fed into the projector. Newer movies are made using digital cameras, and the frames are saved on to a computer.

## Panic station

Early filmgoers were not used to watching motion pictures. It is said that when the film *Train Pulling into a Station*, by Auguste and Louis Lumière, was first shown in Paris in 1896, audiences were scared by the image of a life-sized train moving towards them and tried to run away.

## High definition

Some new movies are filmed using high-speed cameras that take 60 frames per second. This creates movies with greater detail and smoother movement, but many moviegoers complain that they look too realistic. It seems that many of us like knowing that we're watching a movie, and that it isn't real.

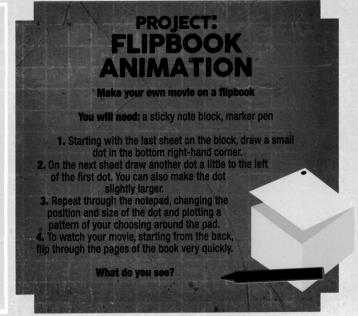

## PROJECT: FLIPBOOK ANIMATION

Make your own movie on a flipbook

**You will need:** a sticky note block, marker pen

1. Starting with the last sheet on the block, draw a small dot in the bottom right-hand corner.
2. On the next sheet draw another dot a little to the left of the first dot. You can also make the dot slightly larger.
3. Repeat through the notepad, changing the position and size of the dot and plotting a pattern of your choosing around the pad.
4. To watch your movie, starting from the back, flip through the pages of the book very quickly.

**What do you see?**

# TURNING ON THE TV

Television was developed in the 1920s as a way to turn radio waves into a moving image on a screen.

## John Logie Baird (1888–1946)

The Scottish inventor John Logie Baird built the first practical TV in 1926. He demonstrated his invention by transmitting the image of a ventriloquist's dummy called Stooky Bill (above).

## Mechanical TV

In the late 1920s, some radio stations began transmitting experimental TV signals. The signals were turned into images by a machine invented by John Logie Baird called a 'televisor'. A spinning metal disc with a series of holes in it passed in front of a neon lamp. Each hole represented one line on the image. The radio signal varied the brightness of the lamp at each point. This created a dim orange image about 4 cm square.

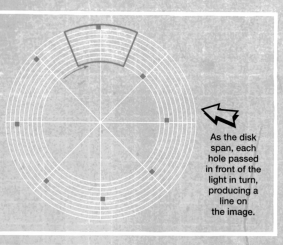

As the disk span, each hole passed in front of the light in turn, producing a line on the image.

# Electronic TV

In the 1930s, electronic TVs replaced Baird's mechanical TV, and the first commercial television stations began broadcasting. Electronic televisions created an image by firing a beam of electrons at a fluorescent screen. The beam scanned across the screen, varying its energy to create different levels of brightness at each point. Modern televisions create an image on the screen from a digital signal.

**Bright spot**

**Magnetic plates deflect electrons to different points on the screen**

**Path of electrons**

**Heated filament gives off a stream of electrons**

**Electrons are focussed and accelerated**

**Fluorescent screen**

# PROJECT:
# RAINBOW SPINNER

At any one moment, just one small section of a television screen is lit, but we see a complete picture if the television scans the screen quickly enough. When objects move quickly enough in front of our eyes, they merge together. You can see this in action with a rainbow spinner.

**You will need:** White cardboard, strong string about 120 cm long, colouring pencils or crayons, sharp pencil, scissors

**1.** Cut out a cardboard disk and divide it into seven equal segments. Colour the segments with the seven colours of the rainbow, as shown.
**2.** Make two holes with the pencil near the centre of the disk about 1 cm apart. Thread the string through the holes, making a loop at each end. Put a finger through the end of each loop and flip the disk over the string several times until the string is well twisted. Now pull your hands apart and let the string go slack. The disk should spin.

**What do you see when the disk spins?**

# SENDING SAFE SIGNALS

Whenever we send a message across technology, there is always the danger that a stranger may be listening in. Creating secret codes to keep messages safe is called encryption. Various methods have been devised to encrypt messages, and today encryption is an essential part of the Internet.

## Hedy Lamarr (1914–2000)

Better known as a film star, Hedy Lamarr was also an ingenious inventor. During the Second World War, she invented a code to protect signals to radio-controlled torpedoes. The radio signals were varied in frequency by adapting a mechanism used for player-pianos. As the frequency was constantly changing, an enemy could not block the signal without knowing the code. Lamarr's invention is now used in Bluetooth and WiFi technology.

## Code breakers

During the Second World War, the German Navy developed a new machine called the Enigma machine to encrypt its messages. The Germans believed that their code was unbreakable, but a team of British cryptographers managed to break it using a machine called the 'Bombe'. Their work remained a secret for many years afterwards.

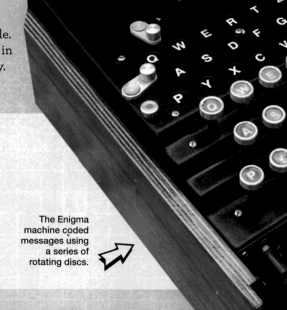

The Enigma machine coded messages using a series of rotating discs.

# Public key encryption

A common method of encryption is called public key encryption. Here's how it works:

**1.** Ally wants to send Jane a costly diamond, but doesn't want it stolen on the way.

**2.** Jane sends Ally an unlocked padlock, for which only Jane has the key.

**3.** Ally puts the diamond in a case and locks it with the padlock.

**4.** On receiving the box, Jane removes the padlock with the key.

Internet encryption works in a very similar way, but in this case, Jane sends out a public key to everybody to use to encrypt their messages, in the form of some digital code. Ally encrypts her message and sends it to Jane, who has the private key needed to decode the message.

# Caesar cypher

Codes have been used to keep secrets for thousands of years. The Roman general Julius Caesar used a code called a substitution cypher to encrypt his messages. He substituted one letter for another letter a fixed number of positions away from it in the alphabet. He wrapped the alphabet around, so that Z came before A. Below is a substitution cypher with each letter substituted for one three back in the alphabet, where E becomes B.

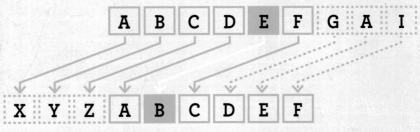

## PROJECT:
# SECRET MESSAGES

When making your own secret messages, it helps to write out the alphabet.

**You will need:** a pen, paper, some friends

**1.** One way to do this is to write the alphabet in 13 rows of two letters, with AB at the top. To substitute with the code (-2), change each letter to the one directly above it. To substitute for (+4), change each letter to the one two rows below. Create your own encrypted messages and see if your friends can decipher them.

## ODOVIN JA OZXCIJGJBT

Cracking codes gets easier with practice. Can you crack this Caesar cypher? What cypher has been used?

# THE WORLD WIDE WEB

By the mid-1980s, computers across the world were linked to one another in a network called the Internet, but there was no easy way to find the information stored on other computers. The World Wide Web allowed computer users to create websites full of information with addresses that other users could search for. Invented in 1989, it marked the start of an information explosion.

### Tim Berners-Lee
### (1955–)

The World Wide Web was invented by the British physicist Tim Berners-Lee. He created the first website in 1991 for the physics research institute CERN, where he was working at the time. The website told visitors how to search the Web and create their own websites. Berners-Lee has campaigned ever since to promote open access to information on the Web.

# Internet explosion

Today, four billion people use the Internet. That's over half the world's population. 700 million people use the Internet in China, which is the country with the most users. There are more than 1.25 billion websites on the Web, with a total of nearly 5 billion pages. To print out the entire web, you would need more than 100 billion pieces of A4 paper.

## PROJECT:
## SEARCH THE WEB

There is an enormous amount of information on the Internet, but not all of it is reliable. Here are a few tips for using search engines.

**You will need:** a computer with Internet connection

WWW.

1. Search engines find results using keywords. The keywords you enter need to be relevant. Put "quotation marks" around a set of words to find an exact match. Put the minus symbol (-) in front of words that you don't want. For example, to find the US presidents except Trump, enter 'US Presidents -Trump'.
2. Once you have the results, the top hits on the page may be the most relevant, but it is worth scrolling down as websites often pay extra to come out at the top.
3. When you select a website, you need to work out if you can trust the information. Domain names (the web addresses) that end in .sch.uk, .ac.uk or .gov.uk are educational websites that are normally reliable. Also look out for organisations such as NASA, who put lots of useful information on the web.
4. Always be critical of what you read. Double-check anything you're not sure of by looking at a trusted website.

Test out different search engines, such as Google, Bing or Yahoo, and compare their results. Which ones do you think work best?

Google is the world's most visited website. More than 5 billion searches are made on Google every day.

# MOBILE PHONE REVOLUTION

Mobile phones allow us to send and receive calls while on the move. Today, more than four billion people own a mobile phone, and many of us never leave home without one.

## John Francis Mitchell (1928–2009)

The idea of a mobile phone network was the brainchild of US phone company Motorola's chief engineer John Mitchell. The first prototype was made in 1973, and mobile phones went on sale to the public ten years later. The first commercially available mobile phone, the DynaTAC 8000X, was 30 centimetres long, weighed nearly 1 kilogram and cost US$4,000. It was nicknamed 'the Brick'.

The first mobile phones were large and heavy. These were replaced in the 1990s by much smaller and lighter models.

Today, many mobiles have become larger again to give them a big screen. Modern smart phones are effectively portable computers.

# How to make a mobile call

Mobile phones can only send signals over short distances. To make a call, you need to send a signal to a nearby phone mast. The call is relayed to the phone mast nearest to the person you are calling, which sends the signal to their phone. To stay in touch, the network needs to know where you are, so your phone sends out a signal as soon as you turn it on.

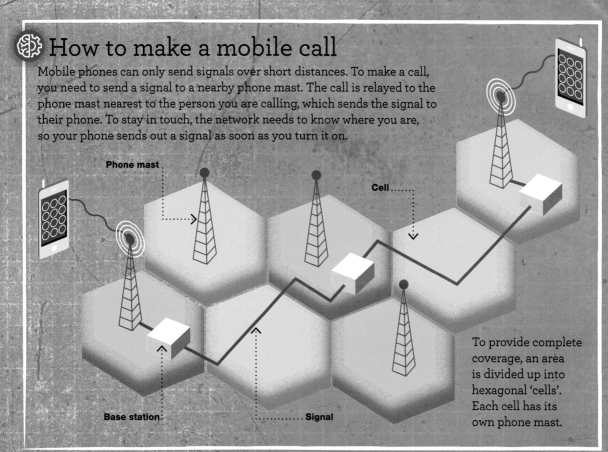

**Phone mast**

**Cell**

**Base station**

**Signal**

To provide complete coverage, an area is divided up into hexagonal 'cells'. Each cell has its own phone mast.

## Satellite phones

You cannot send or receive a call on a mobile phone if you are outside a cell network. Satellite phones work in a similar way to mobile phones, but instead of sending a signal to a phone mast, they send it to a satellite in orbit around Earth. The phones have large antennae to produce a powerful signal. They can send and receive messages from almost anywhere on the planet, and are often carried by people travelling to remote areas.

Satellite phones send messages via a network of satellites in orbit 800 kilometres above Earth.

## PROJECT: NO DISTRACTIONS

Using mobile phones is very distracting, which is why people should never use them while they are driving. Test how distracting they are with this experiment.

**You will need:** a metre stick, test subjects, a stopwatch

**1.** To test your subjects' reactions, hold the metre stick at the 100 cm mark and ask the subject to place their thumb and forefinger around the 0 cm mark. Ask them to catch the stick when you drop it, and record the distance it falls. This is a measure of their reaction time. Perform several trials to produce an average score.
**2.** Repeat the test while the subject is talking on the phone.
**3.** Repeat the test while the subject is texting.

Does using a phone slow reaction times? Which is more distracting, talking or texting?

# FINDING OUR WAY

Today, the Global Positioning System (GPS) has largely replaced maps as the method we use to find our way. We type our destination into the satnav, and it shows us how to get there. It does this by beaming radio signals to satellites in orbit around the planet.

### Roger Easton (1921–2014)

US physicist Roger Easton came up with the idea of a satellite navigation system while working for the US Navy in the 1960s. He called his system Time-Navigation, as it relied on the use of highly accurate clocks. Renamed GPS, it was launched in 1973, initially just for use by the US military. It was made available for civilian use in the 1980s.

The network of GPS satellites provides coverage for almost the entire planet. Each satellite carries a clock that is accurate to within one billionth of a second.

# Satellite system

There are currently 31 GPS satellites in orbit 20,000 km above the ground. A satnav's signal must reach at least four satellites for GPS to find its location. It does this by measuring the time it takes the signal to reach each satellite. This gives the distance from each satellite. GPS calculates the location from these four distances using a process called triangulation.

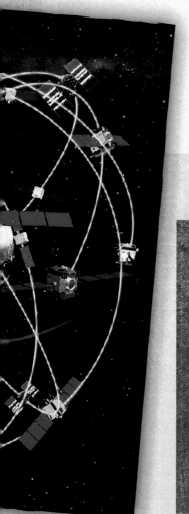

# Triangulation

As its name suggests, triangulation works by creating triangles. In two dimensions, the calculation is simpler. Imagine a hiker trying to reach a friend who is transmitting a signal to him. He does not know how far he will have to walk.

**1.** He can tell what direction the radio waves are coming from but not how far away they are.

**2.** He draws a line to the direction of the signal.

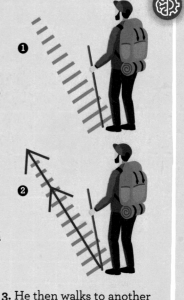

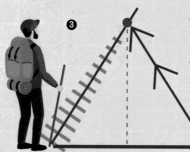

Distance moved

**3.** He then walks to another location and takes a second reading, drawing a line in the new direction of the signal. His friend is at the place where the two lines meet, and he can use the maths technique called trigonometry to work out how far that is.

## PROJECT:
# HUMAN SATNAV

Satnavs need to give accurate instructions to drivers to ensure they stay on route. Turn yourself into a human sat nav and guide a friend from one part of your school to another.

**You will need:** pen and paper, your school

**1.** First you need to record your route. Choose a starting point in your school and an end point in a distant part of the school. Walk the entire route from your starting point, writing down each step of your journey. Arrange your instructions as clearly as you can.

**2.** Start by recording the direction you are facing as you begin your journey. Count the number of steps you take before making your first turn. Describe the angle of the turn and any doors you need to open, then proceed to your next turn. Continue till you reach your destination. At each stage, record how many steps your friend will need to take before the next turn.

**3.** Now hand your instructions over to your friend and take them to the starting point.

**Did they make it to their destination without getting lost?**

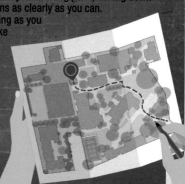

## CYPHER
A method for turning a message into a secret code.

## ELECTROMAGNETIC RADIATION
A form of energy that is transmitted in waves. Light is a kind of electromagnetic radiation.

## ELECTRON
A tiny particle that forms part of the atoms of matter. Electrons have a negative electric charge and flow to produce electricity.

## FILAMENT
A thread-like wire inside a light bulb that glows when an electric current is passed through it.

## FLUORESCENT
A property of a substance that means it glows when electricity or other waves of energy flow through it.

## INFRARED
A form of electromagnetic radiation with a slightly longer wavelength than visible light. Warm objects radiate infrared.

## LED
Short for Light Emitting Diode, a device that gives off light of one particular colour when electricity is passed through it.

## NEON
A gas that can be used to make brightly glowing coloured lights.

## PATENT
A license that gives an inventor sole right to make, use or sell their invention for a period of time.

## PLAYER-PIANO
A self-playing piano that can be programmed to play by means of a roll of perforated paper.

## PROTOTYPE
A model that is made to test a new invention or design.

## STATIC
A crackling noise made by radios or televisions, caused by atmospheric interference.

## TRIGONOMETRY
A branch of mathematics that deals with the properties of triangles.

# ANSWERS

## p.7 Ice cube tray battery
The more cells you add to your battery, the stronger the electric current, so the LED will shine more brightly.

## p.11 Telegraph set
When you touch the copper plate to the screw, you complete an electric circuit. This powers the electromagnet, which pulls the strip above it down to make a click. When you break the circuit, the electromagnet loses its magnetism.

## p.13 Make a light bulb
The iron filament resists the electrical flow and heats up. It should give off a bright red light before burning out. Do not to touch it straight away as it will still be very hot.

## p.15 Make a metal detector
The circuit board of the calculator gives off weak radio waves. Those waves bounce off metal objects and the radio picks them up and amplifies them.

## p.17 Make a string telephone
Your voice vibrates the air inside the cup. The vibrations are transferred to the string and make the air inside your friend's cup vibrate, and they should hear your voice clearly. If the string is slack or being held, the vibrations do not transfer across the string.

## p.19 Flipbook animation
If you flip the book quickly enough, the dot will appear to move around and grow larger and smaller.

## p.23 Secret messages
TITANS OF TECHNOLOGY
The cypher in this case is -5.

## p.21 Rainbow spinner
When you spin the disk, the colours merge together to make the card look white. We see all the colours all over the disk at the same time, and when mixed together, the colours of the rainbow make a white light.

## p.27 Mobile phones
The distracted subjects should have longer reaction times. Texting is usually more distracting than talking.

# INDEX

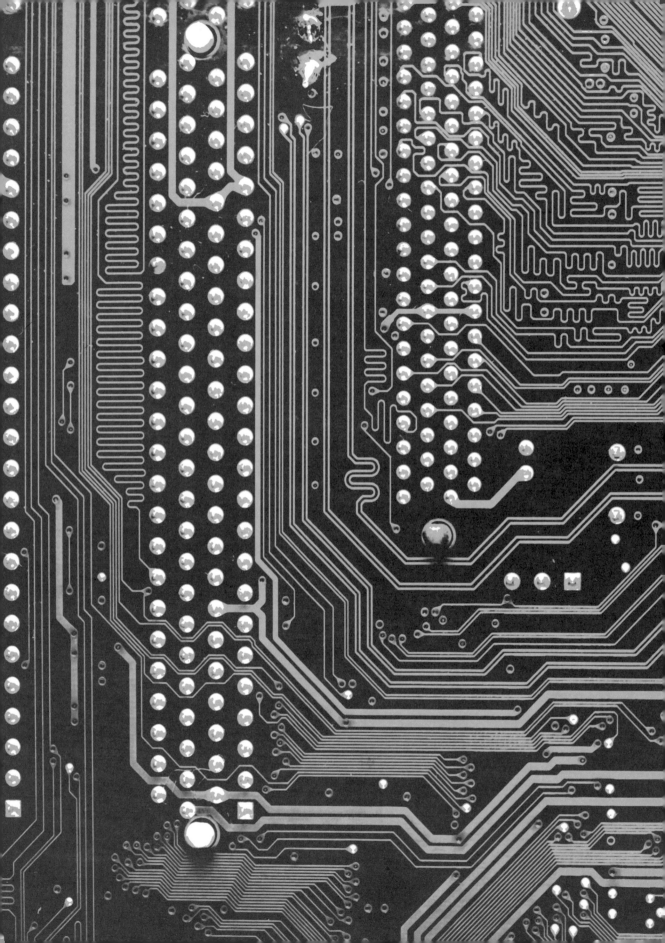